Pyramid Fractions

Fraction Addition and Subtraction Workbook

A Fun Way to Practice
Adding & Subtracting Fractions

Chris McMullen, Ph.D.

Pyramid Fractions – Fraction Addition and Subtraction Workbook: A Fun Way to Practice Adding and Subtracting Fractions

Copyright © 2010 Chris McMullen, Ph.D.

CreateSpace

Nonfiction / Education / Elementary School / Mathematics
Children's / Science / Mathematics / Fractions

ISBN: 1456508903

EAN-13: 978-1456508906

Contents

Introduction

These fraction problems are presented in a creative visual pattern. The idea behind these pyramid fraction problems is for the novelty to engage the interest of young students (and perhaps even some teachers and parents, too). This layout also promotes the development of useful visual skills, too. In this way, students can improve their math fluency and also enjoy doing the math. This format of practicing also ties into a major pedagogical method that has proven teaching effectiveness – visual strategies for learning.

Here is how pyramid math works. There are 21 bricks stacked in a pyramid formation. The 6 bricks in the longest row are filled with fractions. For addition: Start at the second row from the bottom; in each brick, enter the sum of the fractions from the two bricks below it; work your way up to the top of the pyramid. Subtraction works very much the same, except you always subtract the smaller fraction from the larger fraction (from the two bricks below).

The rectangles surrounding the pyramid provide workspace for all of the solutions. The workspaces and answers are all numbered for easy correspondence. The answers to all of the problems are tabulated at the back of the book. The first exercise is partially completed and annotated with instructions in order to help you get started. There are also two completely answered problems on the cover.

May everyone enjoy pyramid fractions! ☺

Mixed Numbers and Improper Fractions

If you want to convert a mixed number to an improper fraction, follow these steps:
1. Multiply the denominator of the mixed number by the whole number out front.
2. Add the numerator of the mixed number to the product you obtained in Step 1.
3. Write your answer from Step 2 over the denominator from the mixed number.

EXAMPLES

$$3\frac{2}{5} = \frac{5 \times 3 + 2}{5} = \frac{15 + 2}{5} = \frac{17}{5} \quad , \quad 5\frac{3}{8} = \frac{8 \times 5 + 3}{8} = \frac{40 + 3}{8} = \frac{43}{8}$$

If you want to convert an improper fraction to a mixed number, follow these steps:
1. Divide the numerator by the denominator using long division.
2. The integer part of the quotient equals the integer part of the mixed number.
3. To get the fractional part, place the remainder over the denominator.

EXAMPLES

$$\frac{13}{4} = 13 \div 4 = 3R1 = 3\frac{1}{4} \quad , \quad \frac{5}{3} = 5 \div 3 = 1R2 = 1\frac{2}{3} \quad , \quad \frac{19}{8} = 19 \div 8 = 2R3 = 2\frac{3}{8}$$

Greatest Common Factor

The **greatest common factor** among two whole numbers is the largest whole number that evenly divides into both of the numbers. For example, the greatest common factor of 12 and 18 is 6: $12 = 6 \times 2$ and $18 = 6 \times 3$.

EXAMPLES

The greatest common factor of 8 and 20 is 4: $8 = 4 \times 2$ and $20 = 4 \times 5$.
The greatest common factor of 15 and 25 is 5: $15 = 5 \times 3$ and $25 = 5 \times 5$.
The greatest common factor of 54 and 72 is **18**: $54 = 18 \times 3$ and $72 = 18 \times 4$.

Reduced Fractions

A proper or improper fraction can be **reduced** if the numerator and denominator share a common factor. To reduce a proper or improper fraction, divide both the numerator and denominator by their greatest common factor.

EXAMPLES

$$\frac{9}{6} = \frac{9 \div 3}{6 \div 3} = \frac{3}{2} \quad , \quad \frac{8}{32} = \frac{8 \div 8}{32 \div 8} = \frac{1}{4} \quad , \quad \frac{36}{27} = \frac{36 \div 9}{27 \div 9} = \frac{4}{3} \quad , \quad \frac{14}{35} = \frac{14 \div 7}{35 \div 7} = \frac{2}{5}$$

Least Common Denominator

To find the **least common denominator** of two fractions, follow these steps:
1. Determine the greatest common factor of the two denominators.
2. Write each denominator in terms of its greatest common factor and another factor.
3. Multiply the greatest common factor times these two other factors.

Two fractions can be expressed with their least common denominator as follows: For each fraction, multiply its numerator and denominator by the factor from the other fraction in Steps 2-3 above. Note that you must multiply both the numerator and denominator by the same factor, but the factor that you use for each fraction will generally be different.

EXAMPLES

Express $\frac{2}{3}$ and $\frac{3}{4}$ with their least common denominator:

The least common denominator is 12:
$$3 = 1 \times 3 \quad , \quad 4 = 1 \times 4 \quad ; \quad 1 \times 3 \times 4 = 12$$

Multiply both the numerator and denominator of $\frac{2}{3}$ by 4.

Multiply both the numerator and denominator of $\frac{3}{4}$ by 3.
$$\frac{2}{3} = \frac{2 \times 4}{3 \times 4} = \frac{8}{12} \quad , \quad \frac{3}{4} = \frac{3 \times 3}{4 \times 3} = \frac{9}{12}$$

Express $\frac{5}{12}$ and $\frac{11}{18}$ with their least common denominator:

The least common denominator is 36:
$$12 = 6 \times 2 \quad , \quad 18 = 6 \times 3 \quad ; \quad 6 \times 2 \times 3 = 36$$

Multiply both the numerator and denominator of $\frac{5}{12}$ by 3.

Multiply both the numerator and denominator of $\frac{11}{18}$ by 2.
$$\frac{5}{12} = \frac{5 \times 3}{12 \times 3} = \frac{15}{36} \quad , \quad \frac{11}{18} = \frac{11 \times 2}{18 \times 2} = \frac{22}{36}$$

Adding Fractions

Two proper and/or improper fractions can be added by first expressing each fraction in terms of their least common denominator and then adding their numerators. If your answer is reducible, cancel the greatest common factor.

EXAMPLES

$$\frac{5}{6} + \frac{4}{9} = \frac{5 \times 3}{6 \times 3} + \frac{4 \times 2}{9 \times 2} = \frac{15}{18} + \frac{8}{18} = \frac{23}{18}$$
$$\frac{5}{12} + \frac{1}{3} = \frac{5 \times 1}{12 \times 1} + \frac{1 \times 4}{12 \times 4} = \frac{5}{12} + \frac{4}{12} = \frac{9}{12} = \frac{3}{4}$$

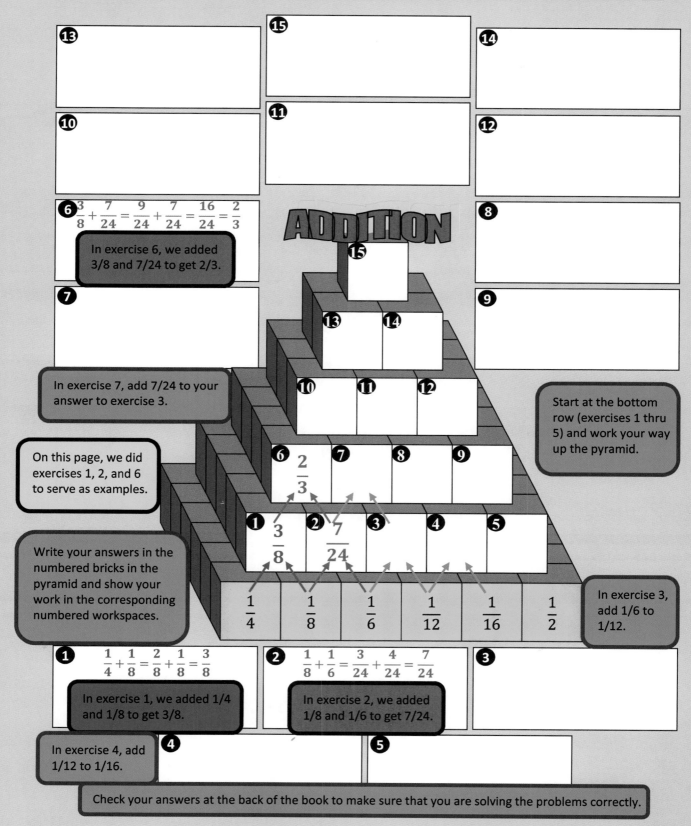

13

15

14

10

11

12

6 $\dfrac{3}{8} + \dfrac{7}{24} = \dfrac{9}{24} + \dfrac{7}{24} = \dfrac{16}{24} = \dfrac{2}{3}$

In exercise 6, we added 3/8 and 7/24 to get 2/3.

8

7

9

ADDITION

In exercise 7, add 7/24 to your answer to exercise 3.

Start at the bottom row (exercises 1 thru 5) and work your way up the pyramid.

On this page, we did exercises 1, 2, and 6 to serve as examples.

15

13 **14**

10 **11** **12**

6 $\dfrac{2}{3}$ **7** **8** **9**

1 $\dfrac{3}{8}$ **2** $\dfrac{7}{24}$ **3** **4** **5**

Write your answers in the numbered bricks in the pyramid and show your work in the corresponding numbered workspaces.

$\dfrac{1}{4}$ $\dfrac{1}{8}$ $\dfrac{1}{6}$ $\dfrac{1}{12}$ $\dfrac{1}{16}$ $\dfrac{1}{2}$

In exercise 3, add 1/6 to 1/12.

1 $\dfrac{1}{4} + \dfrac{1}{8} = \dfrac{2}{8} + \dfrac{1}{8} = \dfrac{3}{8}$

In exercise 1, we added 1/4 and 1/8 to get 3/8.

2 $\dfrac{1}{8} + \dfrac{1}{6} = \dfrac{3}{24} + \dfrac{4}{24} = \dfrac{7}{24}$

In exercise 2, we added 1/8 and 1/6 to get 7/24.

3

In exercise 4, add 1/12 to 1/16.

4

5

Check your answers at the back of the book to make sure that you are solving the problems correctly.

Pyramid Fractions – Fraction Addition and Subtraction Workbook

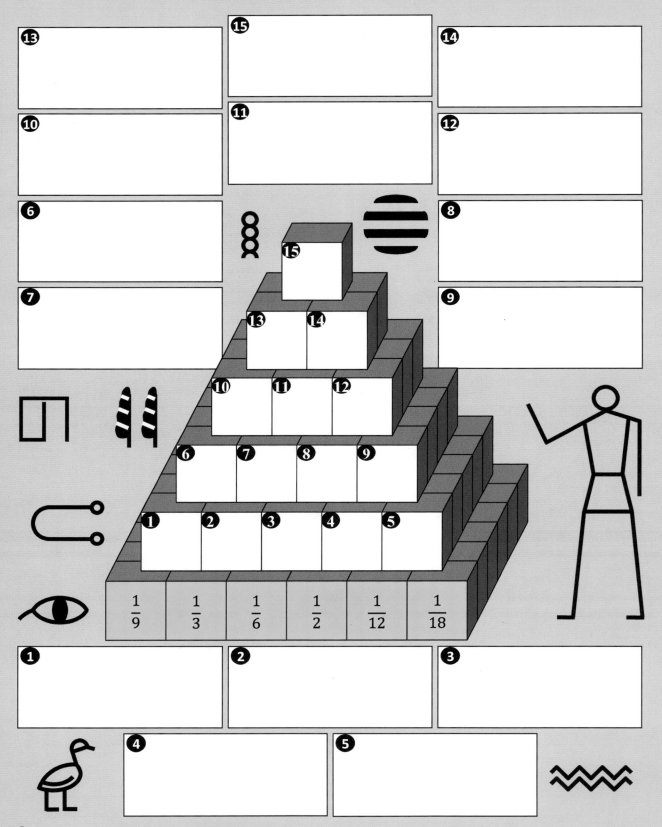

6

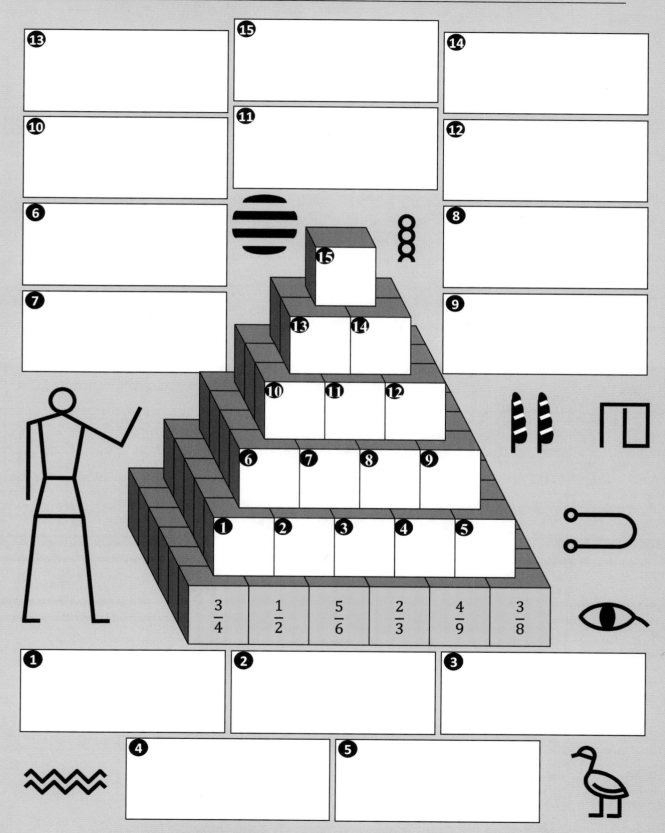

$$\frac{3}{4} \quad \frac{1}{2} \quad \frac{5}{6} \quad \frac{2}{3} \quad \frac{4}{9} \quad \frac{3}{8}$$

7

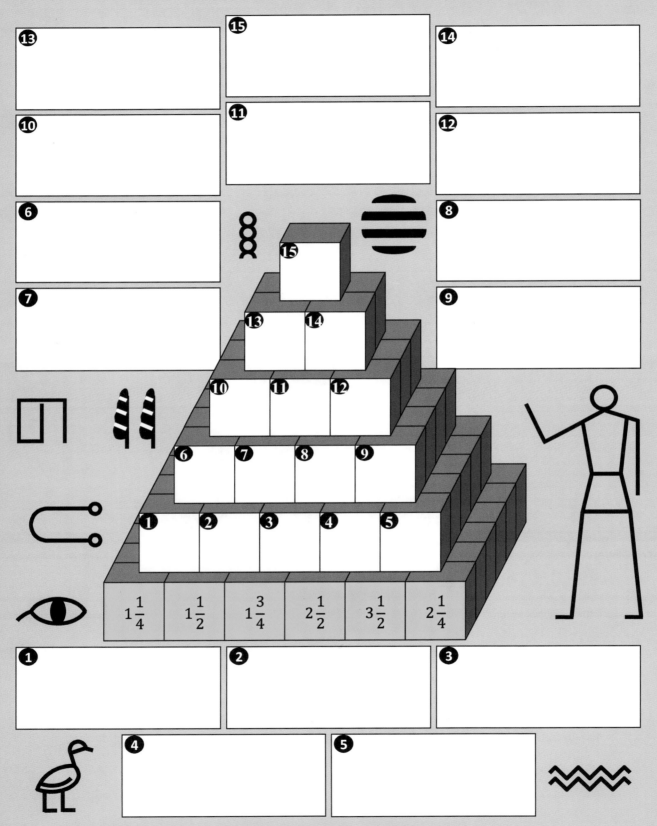

The base row of the pyramid contains the fractions:

$$1\frac{1}{4} \quad 1\frac{1}{2} \quad 1\frac{3}{4} \quad 2\frac{1}{2} \quad 3\frac{1}{2} \quad 2\frac{1}{4}$$

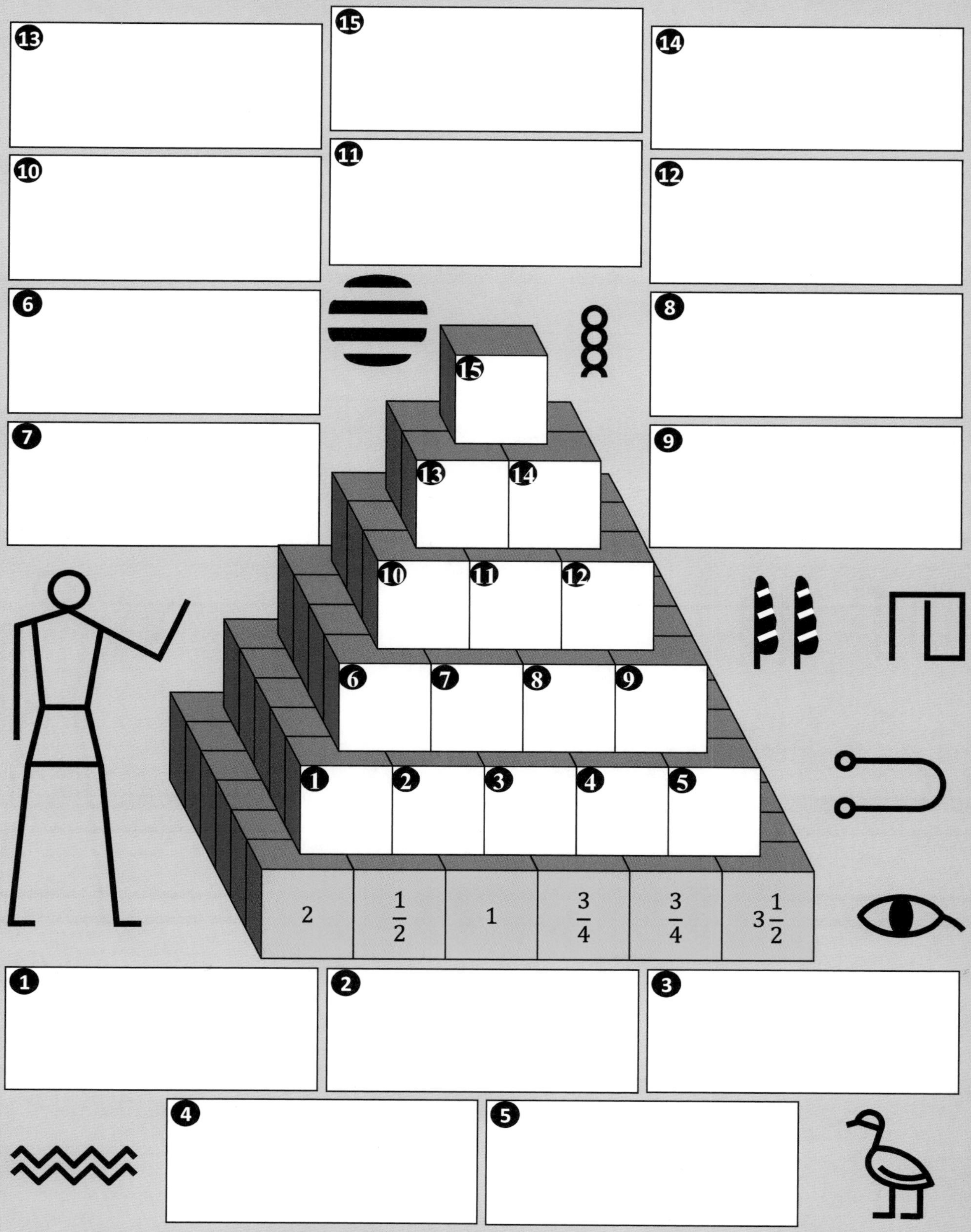

13
15
14
10
11
12
6
8
7
9
15
13
14
10
11
12
6
7
8
9
1
2
3
4
5
2
$\frac{1}{2}$
1
$\frac{3}{4}$
$\frac{3}{4}$
$3\frac{1}{2}$
1
2
3
4
5

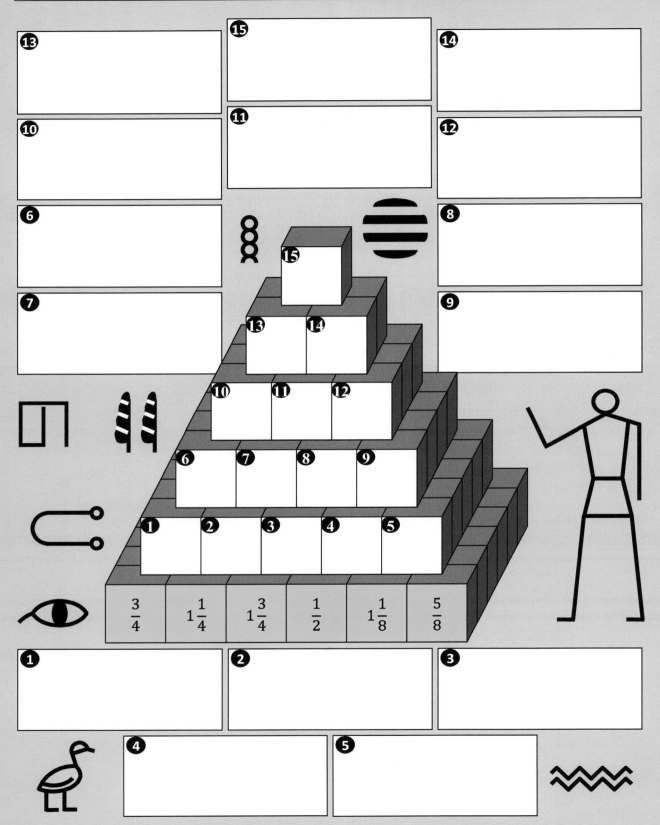

13

15

14

10

11

12

6

8

7

9

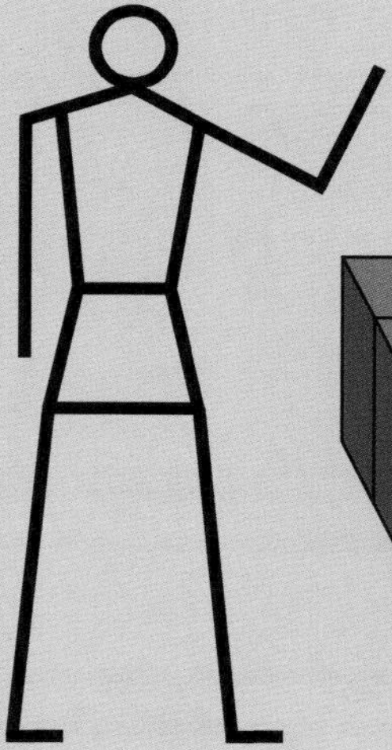

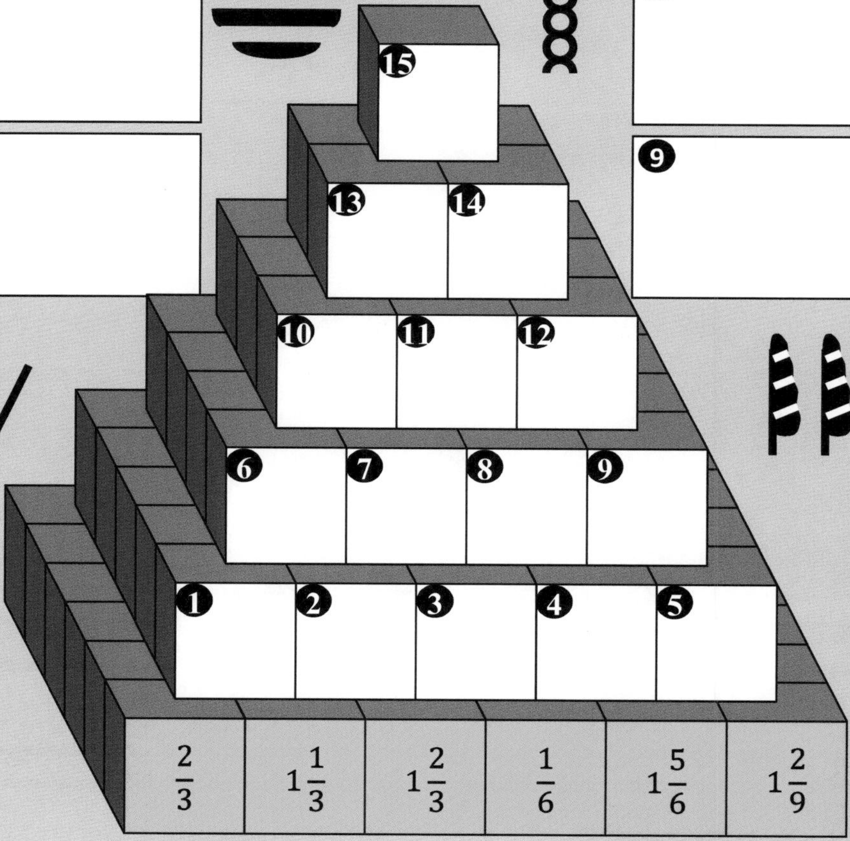
15
13
14
10
11
12
6
7
8
9
1
2
3
4
5
$\frac{2}{3}$
$1\frac{1}{3}$
$1\frac{2}{3}$
$\frac{1}{6}$
$1\frac{5}{6}$
$1\frac{2}{9}$

1

2

3

4

5

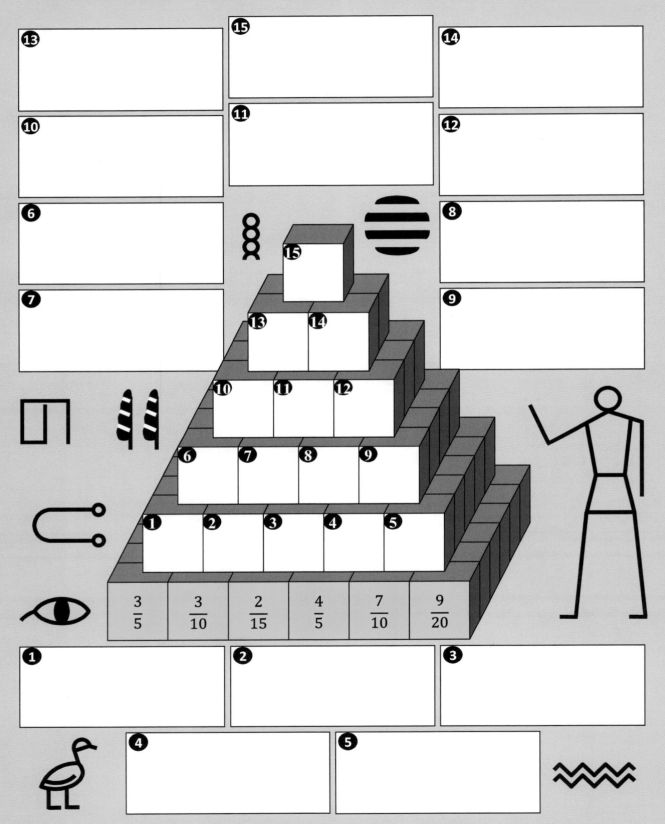

13

15

14

10

11

12

6

8

7

9

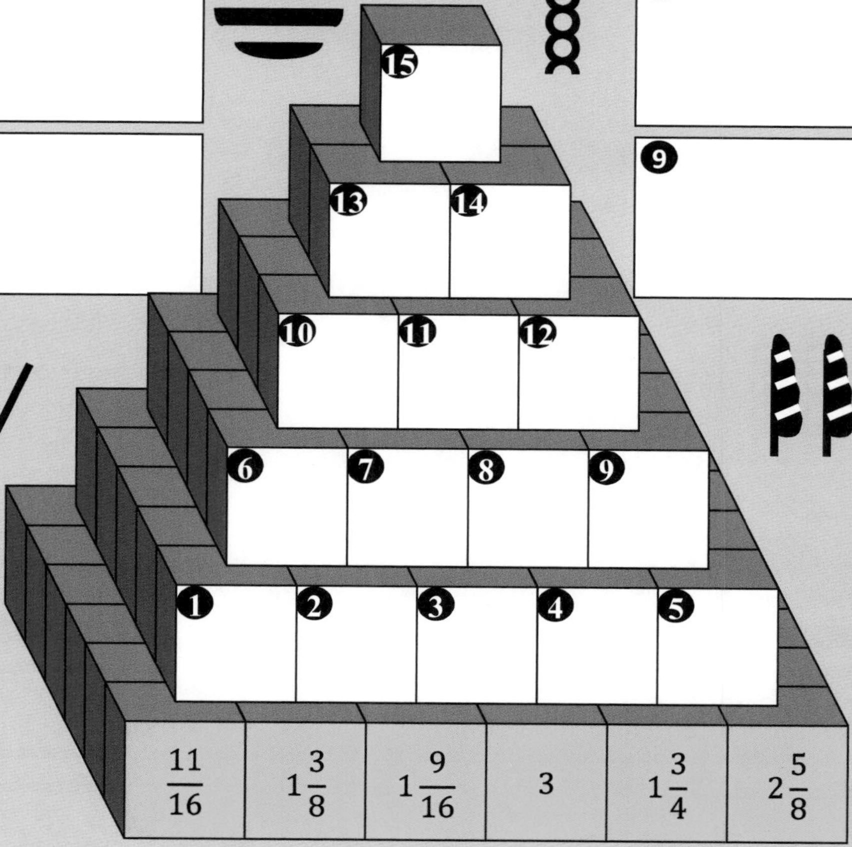
15
13
14
10
11
12
6
7
8
9
1
2
3
4
5
$\frac{11}{16}$
$1\frac{3}{8}$
$1\frac{9}{16}$
3
$1\frac{3}{4}$
$2\frac{5}{8}$

1

2

3

4

5

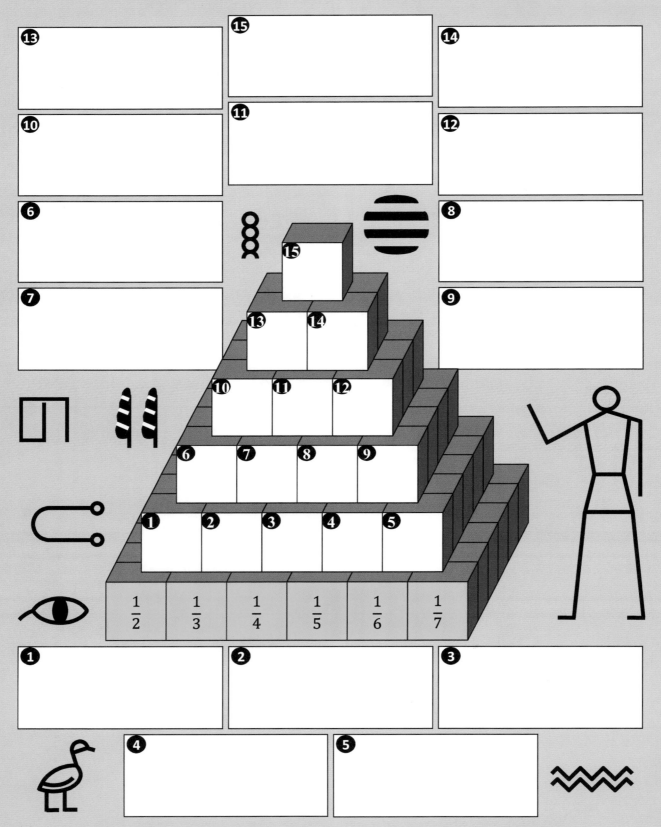

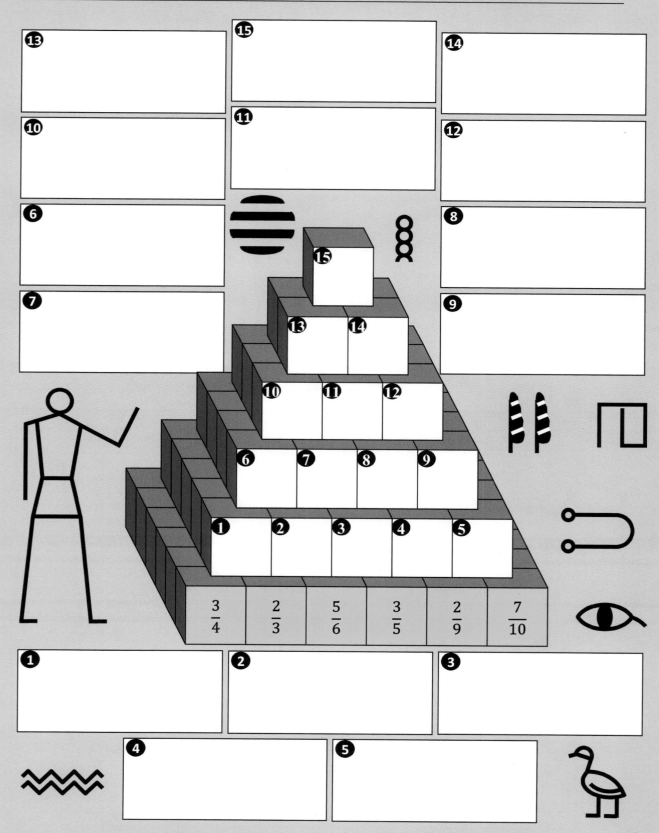

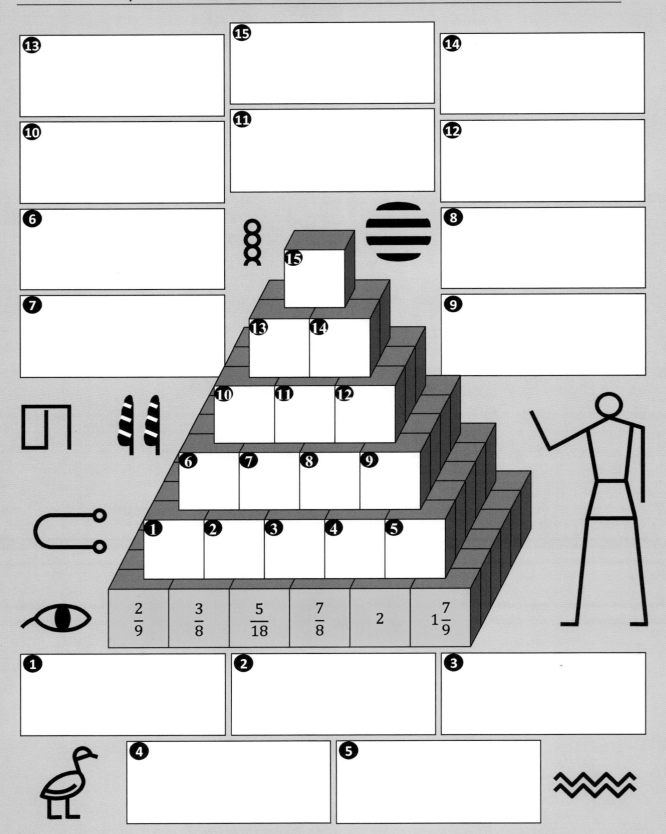

The pyramid base (from left to right):

| $\frac{2}{9}$ | $\frac{3}{8}$ | $\frac{5}{18}$ | $\frac{7}{8}$ | 2 | $1\frac{7}{9}$ |

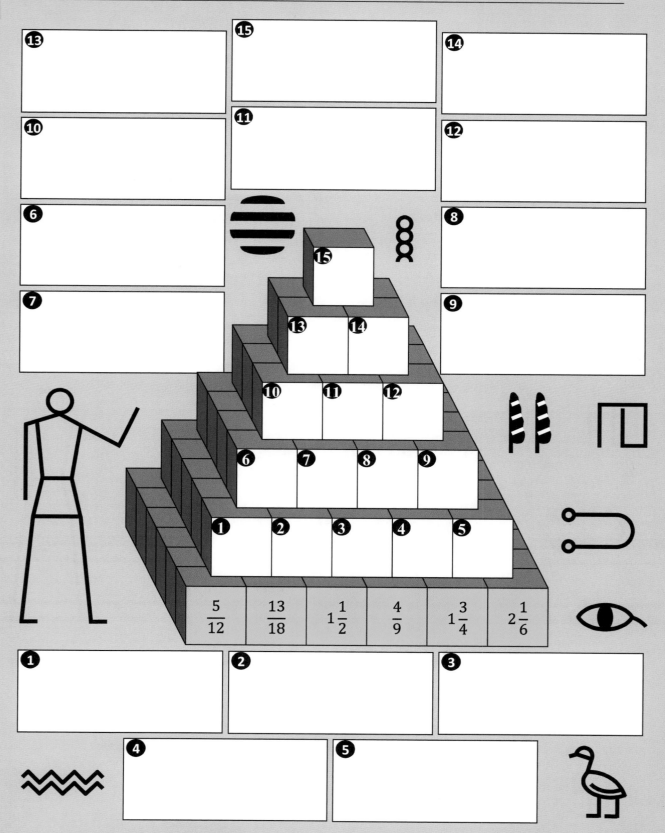

$$\frac{5}{12} \qquad \frac{13}{18} \qquad 1\frac{1}{2} \qquad \frac{4}{9} \qquad 1\frac{3}{4} \qquad 2\frac{1}{6}$$

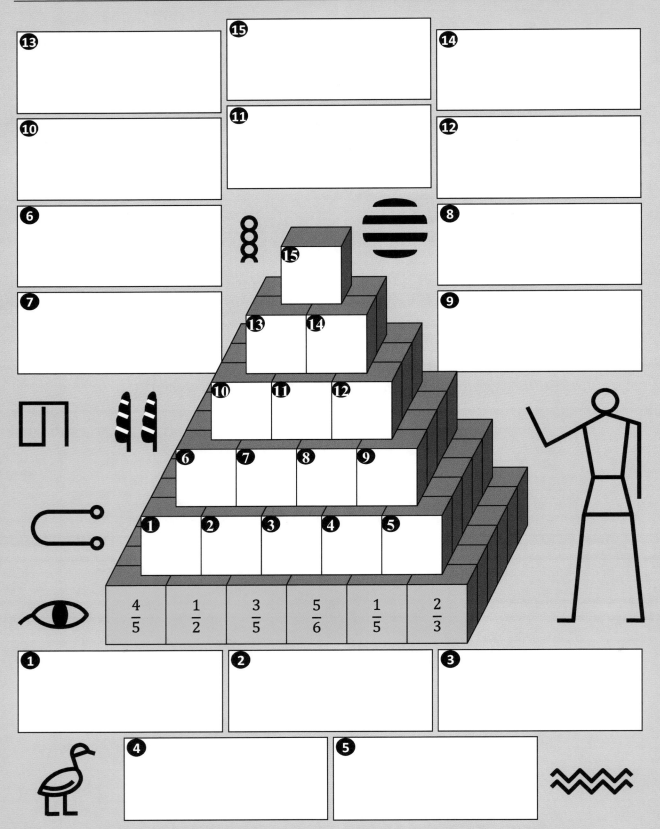

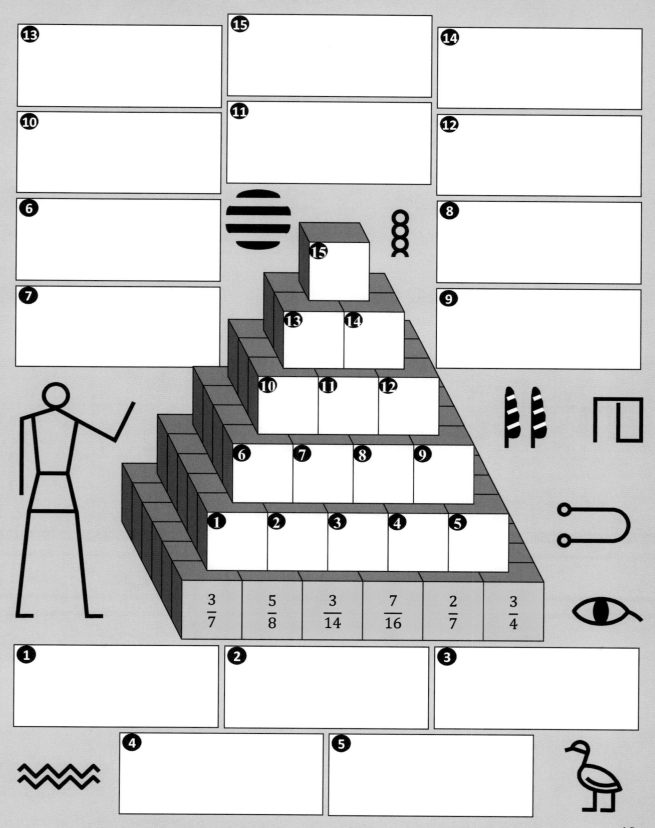

$$\frac{3}{7} \qquad \frac{5}{8} \qquad \frac{3}{14} \qquad \frac{7}{16} \qquad \frac{2}{7} \qquad \frac{3}{4}$$

13

15

14

10

11

12

6

8

7

9

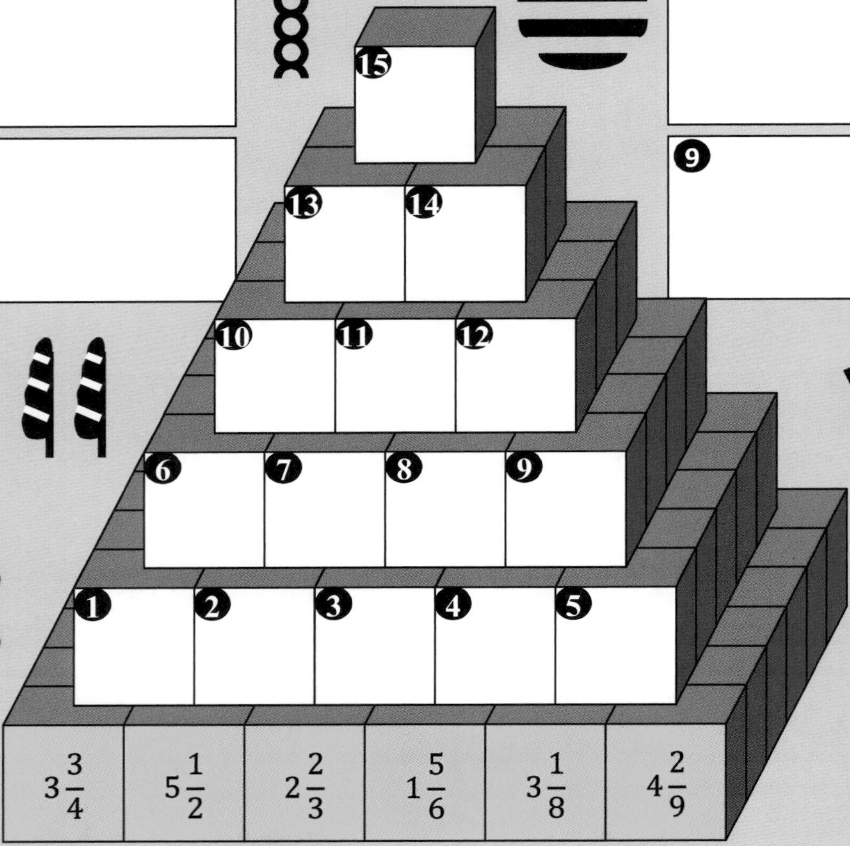
15
13
14
10
11
12
6
7
8
9
1
2
3
4
5
$3\frac{3}{4}$
$5\frac{1}{2}$
$2\frac{2}{3}$
$1\frac{5}{6}$
$3\frac{1}{8}$
$4\frac{2}{9}$

1

2

3

4

5

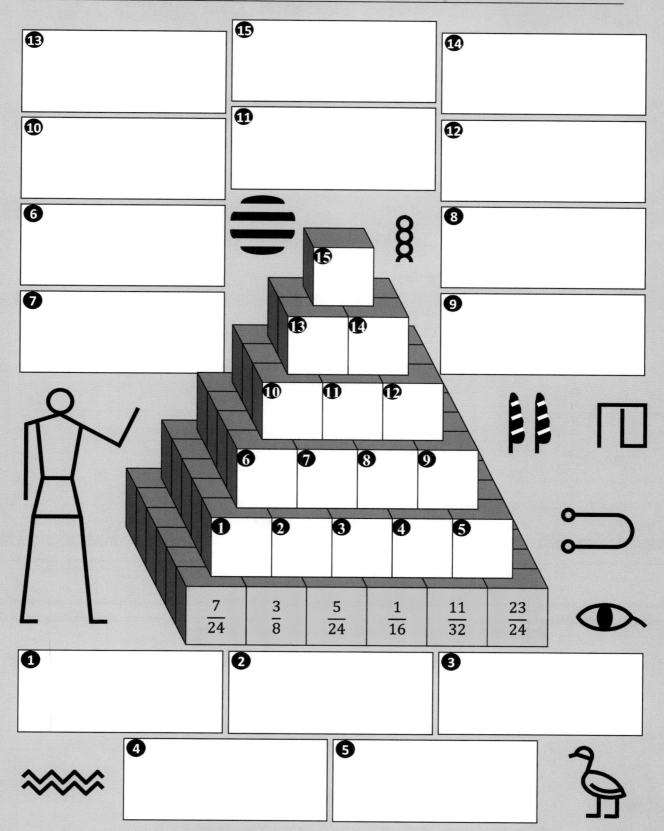

$$\frac{7}{24} \qquad \frac{3}{8} \qquad \frac{5}{24} \qquad \frac{1}{16} \qquad \frac{11}{32} \qquad \frac{23}{24}$$

How to Subtract Fractions

Subtracting Fractions

The strategy for subtracting fractions is almost identical to the strategy for adding fractions: Two proper and/or improper fractions can be subtracted by first expressing each fraction in terms of their least common denominator and then subtracting their numerators. If your answer is reducible, cancel the greatest common factor.

EXAMPLES

$$\frac{5}{6} - \frac{4}{9} = \frac{5 \times 3}{6 \times 3} - \frac{4 \times 2}{9 \times 2} = \frac{15}{18} - \frac{8}{18} = \frac{7}{18}$$

$$\frac{5}{12} - \frac{1}{4} = \frac{5 \times 1}{12 \times 1} - \frac{1 \times 3}{4 \times 3} = \frac{5}{12} - \frac{3}{12} = \frac{2}{12} = \frac{1}{6}$$

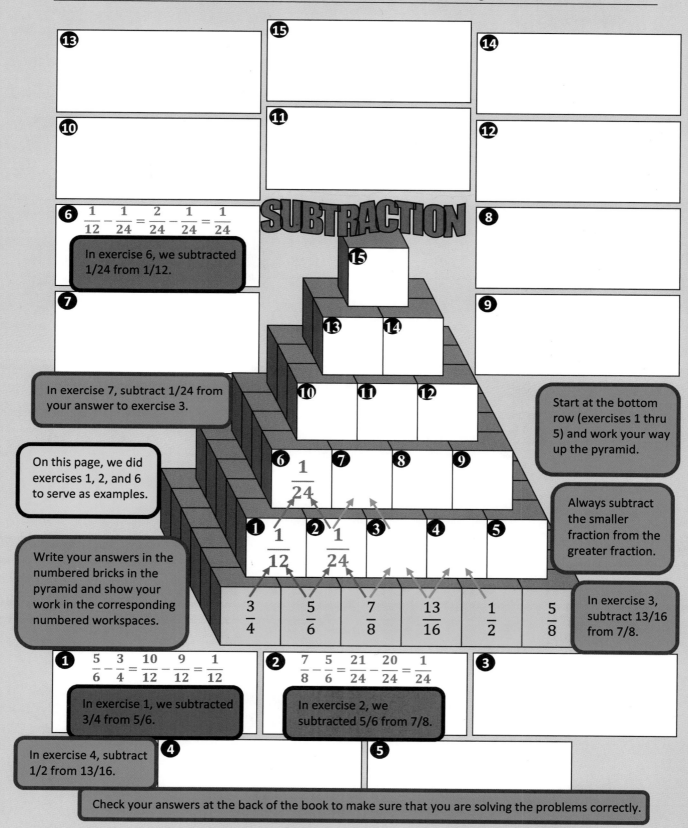

13

15

14

10

11

12

6 $\dfrac{1}{12} - \dfrac{1}{24} = \dfrac{2}{24} - \dfrac{1}{24} = \dfrac{1}{24}$

In exercise 6, we subtracted 1/24 from 1/12.

8

SUBTRACTION

7

In exercise 7, subtract 1/24 from your answer to exercise 3.

9

On this page, we did exercises 1, 2, and 6 to serve as examples.

Start at the bottom row (exercises 1 thru 5) and work your way up the pyramid.

Write your answers in the numbered bricks in the pyramid and show your work in the corresponding numbered workspaces.

Always subtract the smaller fraction from the greater fraction.

In exercise 3, subtract 13/16 from 7/8.

$\dfrac{15}{}$

$\dfrac{13}{}$ $\dfrac{14}{}$

$\dfrac{10}{}$ $\dfrac{11}{}$ $\dfrac{12}{}$

$\dfrac{6}{} \dfrac{1}{24}$ $\dfrac{7}{}$ $\dfrac{8}{}$ $\dfrac{9}{}$

$\dfrac{1}{} \dfrac{1}{12}$ $\dfrac{2}{} \dfrac{1}{24}$ $\dfrac{3}{}$ $\dfrac{4}{}$ $\dfrac{5}{}$

$\dfrac{3}{4}$ $\dfrac{5}{6}$ $\dfrac{7}{8}$ $\dfrac{13}{16}$ $\dfrac{1}{2}$ $\dfrac{5}{8}$

1 $\dfrac{5}{6} - \dfrac{3}{4} = \dfrac{10}{12} - \dfrac{9}{12} = \dfrac{1}{12}$

In exercise 1, we subtracted 3/4 from 5/6.

2 $\dfrac{7}{8} - \dfrac{5}{6} = \dfrac{21}{24} - \dfrac{20}{24} = \dfrac{1}{24}$

In exercise 2, we subtracted 5/6 from 7/8.

3

In exercise 4, subtract 1/2 from 13/16.

4

5

Check your answers at the back of the book to make sure that you are solving the problems correctly.

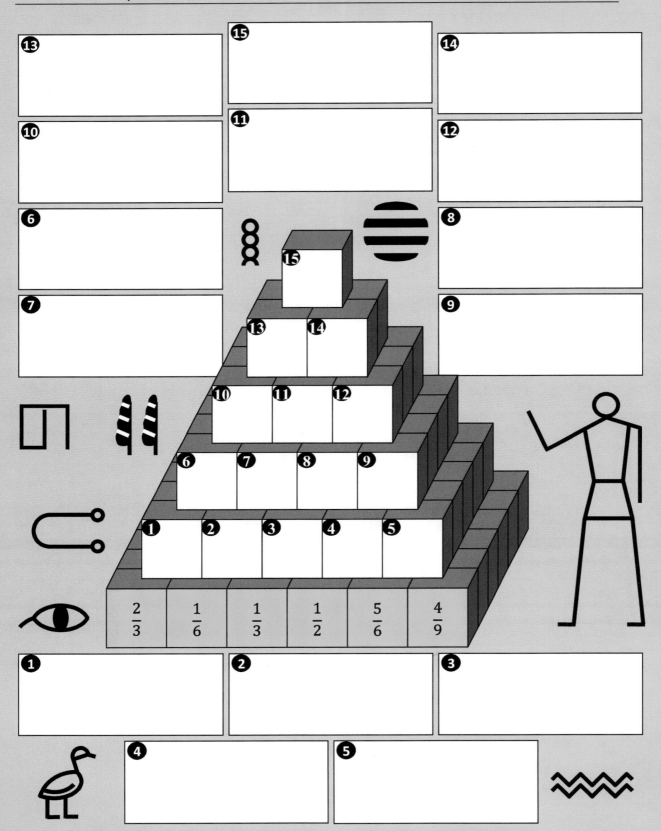

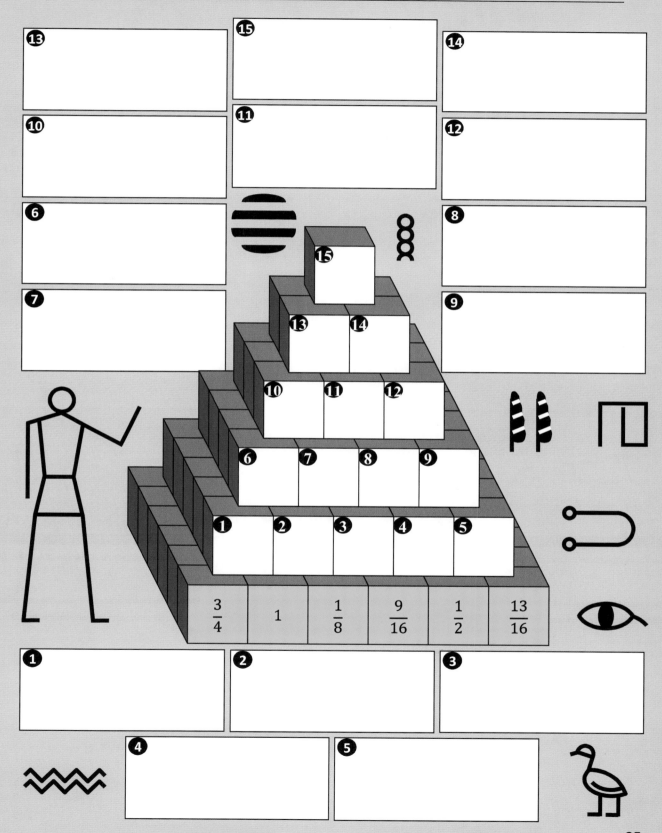

$$\frac{3}{4} \qquad 1 \qquad \frac{1}{8} \qquad \frac{9}{16} \qquad \frac{1}{2} \qquad \frac{13}{16}$$

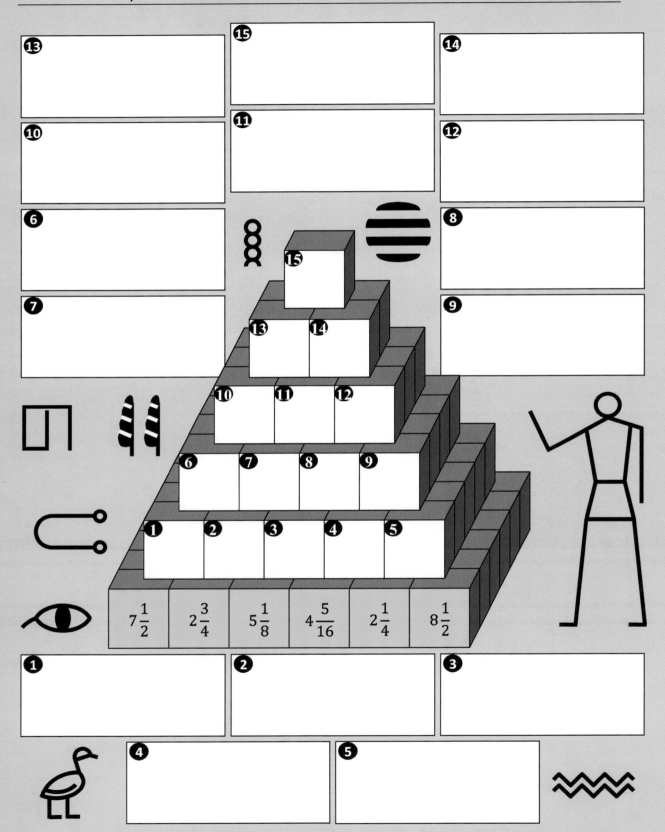

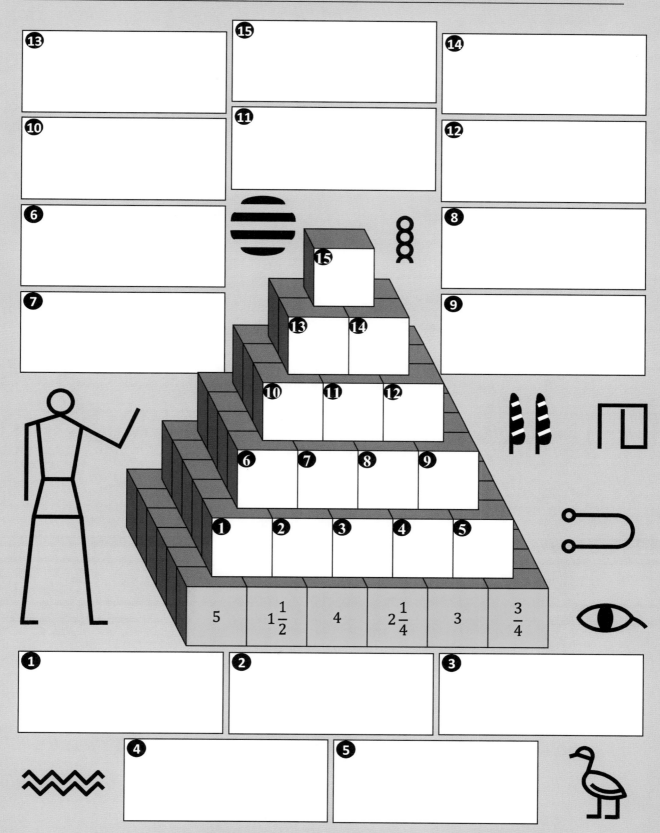

The base row values: 5, $1\frac{1}{2}$, 4, $2\frac{1}{4}$, 3, $\frac{3}{4}$

13

15

14

10

11

12

6

8

7

9

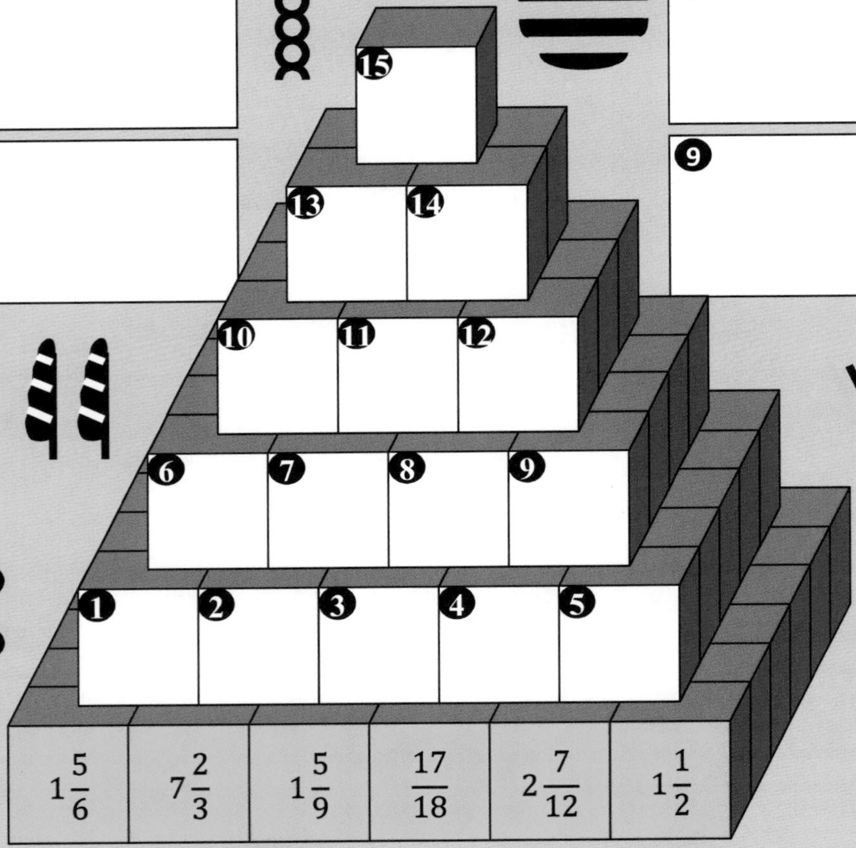
15
13
14
10
11
12
6
7
8
9
1
2
3
4
5
$1\frac{5}{6}$
$7\frac{2}{3}$
$1\frac{5}{9}$
$\frac{17}{18}$
$2\frac{7}{12}$
$1\frac{1}{2}$

1

2

3

4

5

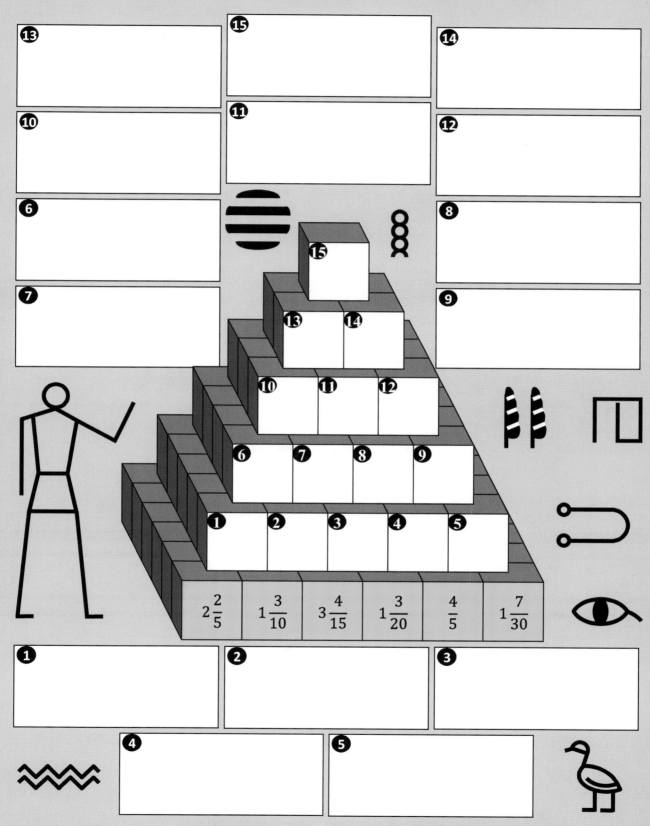

13

15

14

10

11

12

6

8

7

9

Pyramid blocks:

15

13 **14**

10 **11** **12**

6 **7** **8** **9**

1 **2** **3** **4** **5**

Base row:

| $2\frac{2}{5}$ | $1\frac{3}{10}$ | $3\frac{4}{15}$ | $1\frac{3}{20}$ | $\frac{4}{5}$ | $1\frac{7}{30}$ |

1

2

3

4

5

29

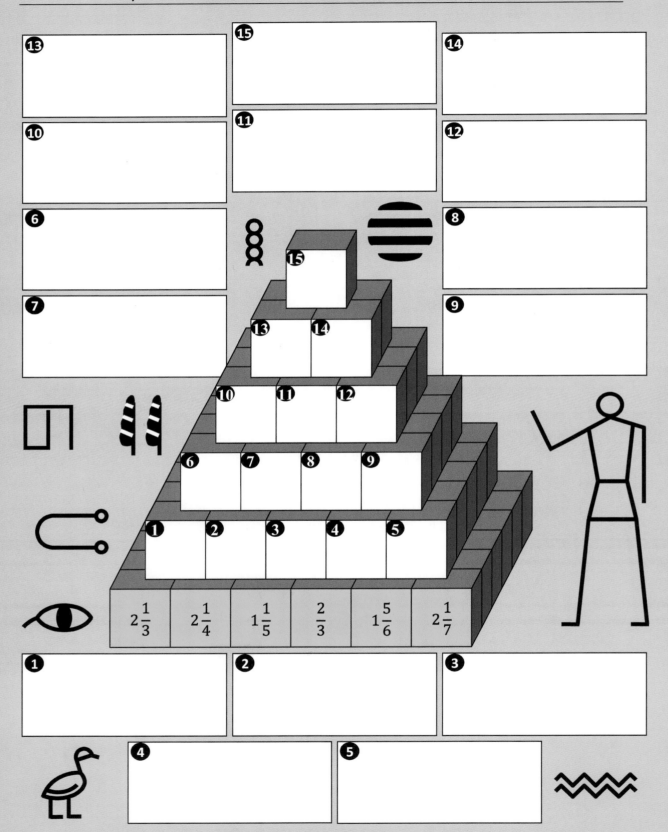

2⅓ 2¼ 1⅕ ⅔ 1⅚ 2⅐

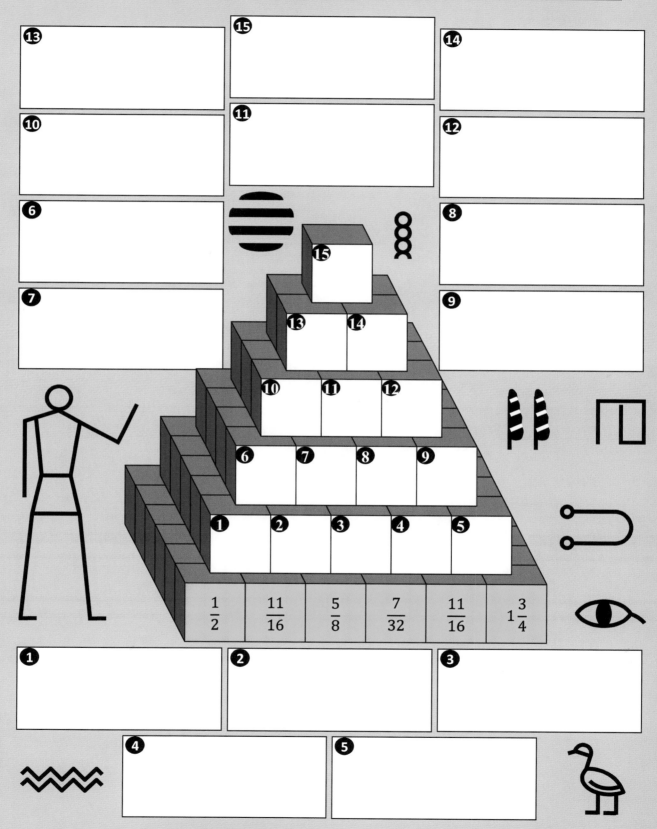

Bottom row of pyramid:

| $\frac{1}{2}$ | $\frac{11}{16}$ | $\frac{5}{8}$ | $\frac{7}{32}$ | $\frac{11}{16}$ | $1\frac{3}{4}$ |

13

15

14

10

11

12

6

8

7

9

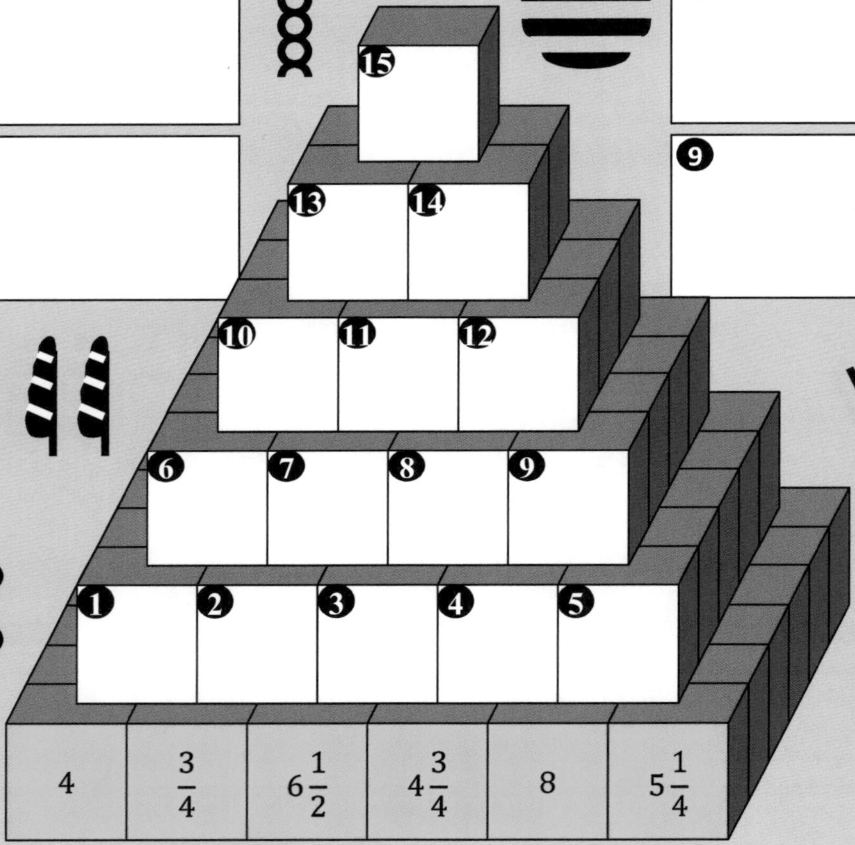

1

2

3

4

5

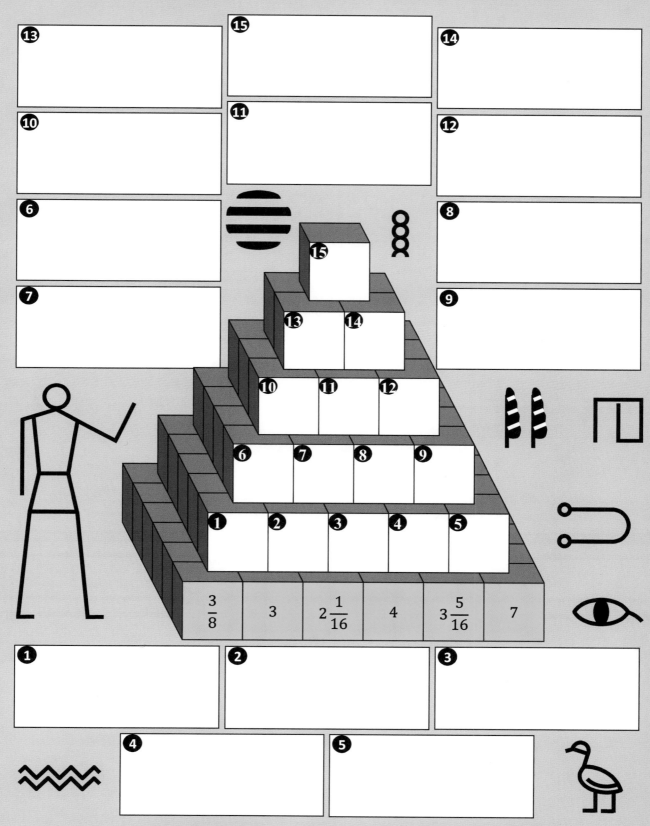

The base row of the pyramid contains:

$\frac{3}{8}$	3	$2\frac{1}{16}$	4	$3\frac{5}{16}$	7

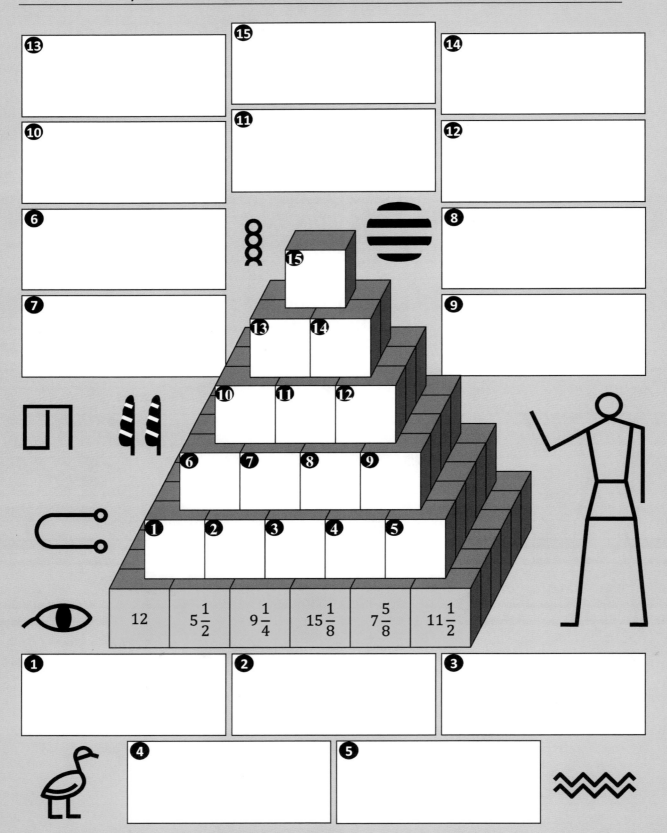

13

15

14

10

11

12

6

8

7

9

| 12 | $5\frac{1}{2}$ | $9\frac{1}{4}$ | $15\frac{1}{8}$ | $7\frac{5}{8}$ | $11\frac{1}{2}$ |

1

2

3

4

5

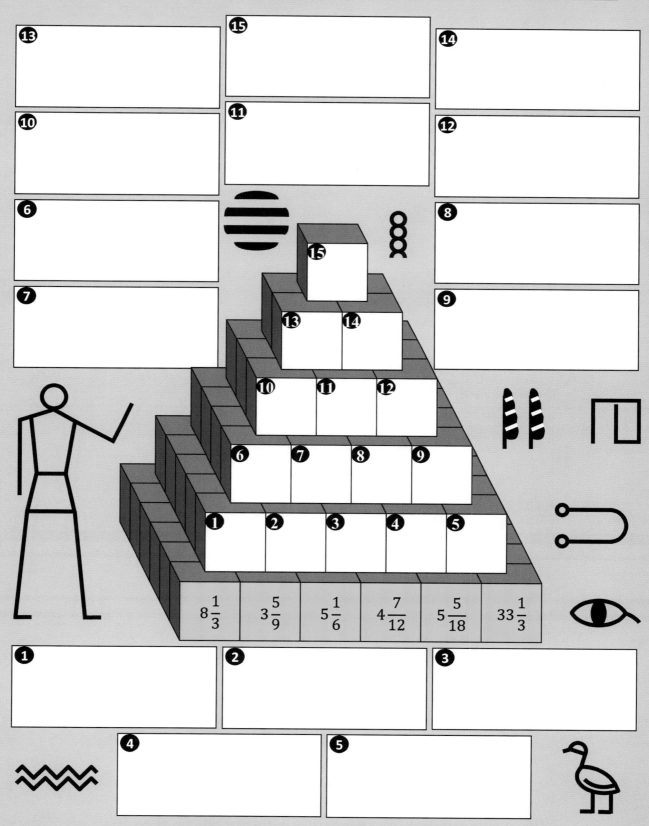

The base row of the pyramid shows:

$8\frac{1}{3}$	$3\frac{5}{9}$	$5\frac{1}{6}$	$4\frac{7}{12}$	$5\frac{5}{18}$	$33\frac{1}{3}$

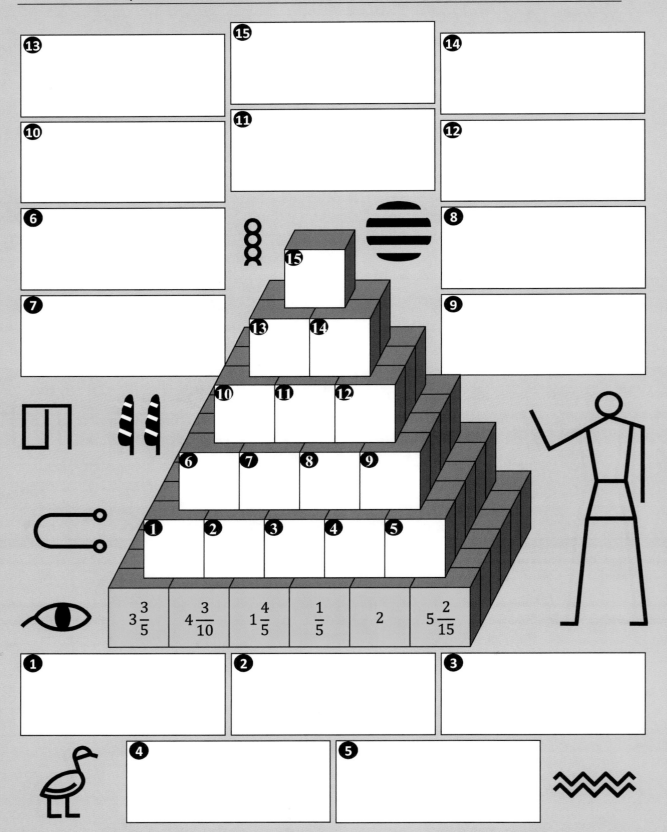

$3\frac{3}{5}$ $4\frac{3}{10}$ $1\frac{4}{5}$ $\frac{1}{5}$ 2 $5\frac{2}{15}$

13

15

14

10

11

12

6

8

7

9

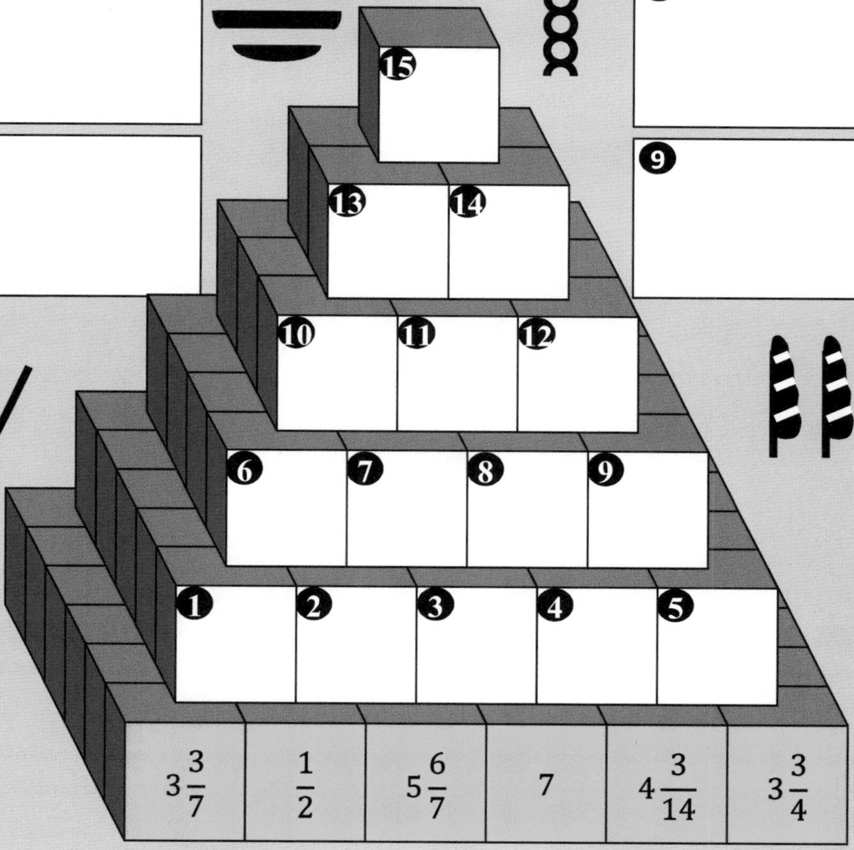
15
13
14
10
11
12
6
7
8
9
1
2
3
4
5
$3\frac{3}{7}$
$\frac{1}{2}$
$5\frac{6}{7}$
7
$4\frac{3}{14}$
$3\frac{3}{4}$

1

2

3

4

5

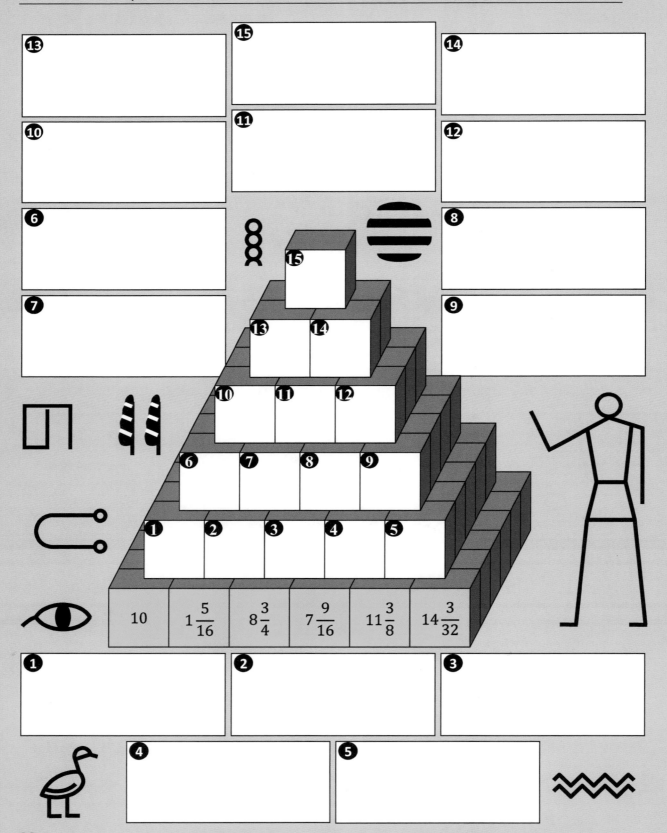

| 10 | $1\frac{5}{16}$ | $8\frac{3}{4}$ | $7\frac{9}{16}$ | $11\frac{3}{8}$ | $14\frac{3}{32}$ |

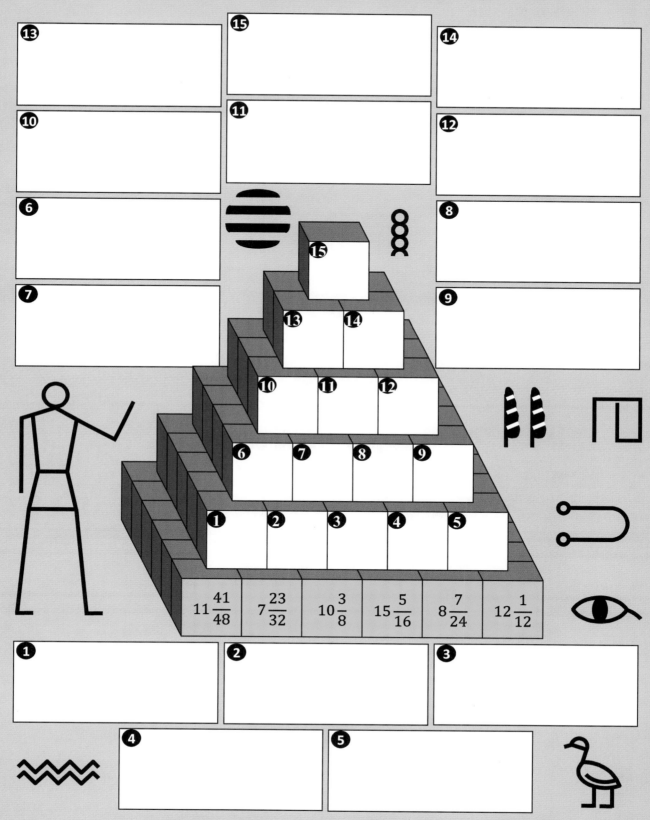

$$11\frac{41}{48} \quad 7\frac{23}{32} \quad 10\frac{3}{8} \quad 15\frac{5}{16} \quad 8\frac{7}{24} \quad 12\frac{1}{12}$$

Addition Answers

Page 5	3/8	7/24	1/4	7/48	9/16	2/3	13/24	19/48	17/24	1 5/24	15/16	1 5/48	2 7/48	2 1/24	4 3/16
Page 6	4/9	1/2	2/3	7/12	5/36	17/18	1 1/6	1 1/4	13/18	2 1/9	2 5/12	1 35/36	4 19/36	4 7/18	8 11/12
Page 7	1 1/4	1 1/3	1 1/2	1 1/9	59/72	2 7/12	2 5/6	2 11/18	1 67/72	5 5/12	5 4/9	4 13/24	10 31/36	9 71/72	20 61/72
Page 8	2 3/4	3 1/4	4 1/4	6	5 3/4	6	7 1/2	10 1/4	11 3/4	13 1/2	17 3/4	22	31 1/4	39 3/4	71
Page 9	2 1/2	1 1/2	1 3/4	1 1/2	4 1/4	4	3 1/4	3 1/4	5 3/4	7 1/4	6 1/2	9	13 3/4	15 1/2	29 1/4
Page 10	2	3	2 1/4	1 5/8	1 3/4	5	5 1/4	3 7/8	3 3/8	10 1/4	9 1/8	7 1/4	19 3/8	16 3/8	35 3/4
Page 11	2	3	1 5/6	2	3 1/18	5	4 5/6	3 5/6	5 1/18	9 5/6	8 2/3	8 8/9	18 1/2	17 5/9	36 1/18
Page 12	9/10	13/30	14/15	1 1/2	1 3/20	1 1/3	1 11/30	2 13/30	2 13/20	2 7/10	3 4/5	5 1/12	6 1/2	8 53/60	15 23/60
Page 13	2 1/16	2 15/16	4 9/16	4 3/4	4 3/8	5	7 1/2	9 5/16	9 1/8	12 1/2	16 13/16	18 7/16	29 5/16	35 1/4	64 9/16
Page 14	5/6	7/12	9/20	11/30	13/42	1 5/12	1 1/30	49/60	71/105	2 9/20	1 17/20	1 69/140	4 3/10	3 12/35	7 9/14
Page 15	1 5/12	1 1/2	1 13/30	37/45	83/90	2 11/12	2 14/15	2 23/90	1 67/90	5 17/20	5 17/90	4	11 7/180	9 17/90	20 41/180
Page 16	43/72	47/72	1 11/72	2 7/8	3 7/9	1 1/4	1 29/36	4 1/36	6 47/72	3 1/18	5 5/6	10 49/72	8 8/9	16 37/72	25 29/72
Page 17	1 5/36	2 2/9	1 17/18	2 7/36	3 11/12	3 13/36	4 1/6	4 5/36	6 1/9	7 19/36	8 11/36	10 1/4	15 5/6	18 5/9	34 7/18
Page 18	1 3/10	1 1/10	1 13/30	1 1/30	13/15	2 2/5	2 8/15	2 7/15	1 9/10	4 14/15	5	4 11/30	9 14/15	9 11/30	19 3/10
Page 19	1 3/56	47/56	73/112	81/112	1 1/28	1 25/28	1 55/112	1 3/8	1 85/112	3 43/112	2 97/112	3 15/112	6 1/4	6	12 1/4
Page 20	9 1/4	8 1/6	4 1/2	4 23/24	7 25/72	17 5/12	12 2/3	9 11/24	12 11/36	30 1/12	22 1/8	21 55/72	52 5/24	43 8/9	96 7/72
Page 21	2/3	7/12	13/48	13/32	1 29/96	1 1/4	41/48	65/96	1 17/24	2 5/48	1 17/32	2 37/96	3 61/96	3 11/12	7 53/96

Subtraction Answers

Page 23	1/12	1/24	1/16	5/16	1/8	1/24	1/48	1/4	3/16	1/48	11/48	1/16	5/24	1/6	1/24
Page 24	1/2	1/6	1/6	1/3	7/18	1/3	0	1/6	1/18	1/3	1/6	1/9	1/6	1/18	1/9
Page 25	1/4	7/8	7/16	1/16	5/16	5/8	7/16	3/8	1/4	3/16	1/16	1/8	1/8	1/16	1/16
Page 26	4 3/4	2 3/8	13/16	2 1/16	6 1/4	2 3/8	1 9/16	1 1/4	4 3/16	13/16	5/16	2 15/16	1/2	2 5/8	2 1/8
Page 27	3 1/2	2 1/2	1 3/4	3/4	2 1/4	1	3/4	1	1 1/2	1/4	1/4	1/2	0	1/4	1/4
Page 28	5 5/6	6 1/9	11/18	1 23/36	1 1/12	5/18	5 1/2	1 1/36	5/9	5 2/9	4 17/36	17/36	3/4	4	3 1/4
Page 29	1 1/10	1 29/30	2 7/60	7/20	13/30	13/15	3/20	1 23/30	1/12	43/60	1 37/60	1 41/60	9/10	1/15	5/6
Page 30	1/12	1 1/20	8/15	1 1/6	13/42	29/30	31/60	19/30	6/7	9/20	7/60	47/210	1/3	3/28	19/84
Page 31	3/16	1/16	13/32	15/32	1 1/16	1/8	11/32	1/16	19/32	7/32	9/32	17/32	1/16	1/4	3/16
Page 32	3 1/4	5 3/4	1 3/4	3 1/4	2 3/4	2 1/2	4	1 1/2	1/2	1 1/2	2 1/2	1	1	1 1/2	1/2
Page 33	2 5/8	15/16	1 15/16	11/16	3 11/16	1 11/16	1	1 1/4	3	11/16	1/4	1 3/4	7/16	1 1/2	1 1/16
Page 34	6 1/2	3 3/4	5 7/8	7 1/2	3 7/8	2 3/4	2 1/8	1 5/8	3 5/8	5/8	1/2	2	1/8	1 1/2	1 3/8
Page 35	4 7/9	1 11/18	7/12	25/36	28 1/18	3 1/6	1 1/36	1/9	27 13/36	2 5/36	11/12	27 1/4	1 2/9	26 1/3	25 1/9
Page 36	7/10	2 1/2	1 3/5	1 4/5	3 2/15	1 4/5	9/10	1/5	1 1/3	9/10	7/10	1 2/15	1/5	13/30	7/30
Page 37	2 13/14	5 5/14	1 1/7	2 11/14	13/28	2 3/7	4 3/14	1 9/14	2 9/28	1 11/14	2 4/7	19/28	11/14	1 25/28	1 3/28
Page 38	8 11/16	7 7/16	1 3/16	3 13/16	2 23/32	1 1/4	6 1/4	2 5/8	1 3/32	5	3 5/8	1 17/32	1 3/8	2 3/32	23/32
Page 39	4 13/96	2 21/32	4 15/16	7 1/48	3 19/24	1 23/48	2 9/32	2 1/12	3 11/48	77/96	19/96	1 7/48	29/48	91/96	11/32